Pet Owner's Guide to
THE
ROTTWEILER

Mary Macphail

RINGPRESS

RINGPRESS

Published by Ringpress Books Limited,
Spirella House, Bridge Road,
Letchworth, Herts, United Kingdom, SG6 4ET.

First Published 1993
© 1993 Ringpress Books Limited.
All rights reserved

ISBN 0 948955 38 4

Printed and bound in Hong Kong

Contents

*A memory
for 'Jax'*

About the author

Mary Macphail owned her first Rottweiler in 1958 and since then she has bred, exhibited and judged the breed with great success. She is an international Championship Show judge, and she has judged Rottweilers at Crufts on two occasions, including the Crufts Centenary Show. Mrs Macphail has now judged the Rottweiler in twelve different countries, including the USA, Canada, Australia, New Zealand, Norway, Holland and Israel. She has also judged the breed in Germany, and she is the only person in Britain who is qualified to judge the Rottweiler in its country of origin. Mrs Macphail has written for the English weekly dog paper *Dog World* for the last twenty years.

Acknowledgements

I want to express my thanks to the many people who have helped me with this book with suggestions, photographs, and lending support. Alas, it is not possible to mention them all, but special thanks must go to Roy Hunter, Hilary Jupp, Elizabeth Kershaw and Liz Harrap for suggestions on the text; Dick Delany for photographic contributions; Stagecoach (Hants and Surrey), the Watercress Line and Blackbushe Airport for allowing us to use their locations, and the Kentish Express for the photograph on page 45.

Special thanks to Muriel Brendon (and daughters Jude and Liz), Dave and Roni Parish, Christine Blance and Ann Garside-Neville for their help with photographs – and to all models – human and canine – who showed such patience.

*Jacket photograph: Fantasa Red Hot Lover (pet name George).
Owned by Fred Baker. Bred by Liz and John Dunhill.*

Chapter One

CHOOSING A ROTTWEILER

ORIGINS OF THE BREED
The Rottweiler takes its name from the German town of Rottweil in the Black Forest. The breed is thought to have evolved from the mixing together of Roman herding dogs, who travelled with the legions over the Alps, native cattle dogs, and broad-mouthed forms of British and Dutch Bulldogs.

With the coming of the railways, the driving of cattle was forbidden by law, but the Rottweiler gained a new occupation – pulling butchers' small carts. In time, this work also became obsolete, and the Rottweiler's future looked bleak. Then, in 1910 the breed was recognised as a police dog, joining the German Shepherd Dog, Dobermann and Airedale, and it has since gone from strength to strength, gaining worldwide recognition.

In 1931 the first Rottweilers were imported into the United States, and five years later the breed was introduced to the UK. The Second World War severely restricted breeding, but when this situation eased, numbers began to increase. This growth was not meteoric; it took place gradually, until the breed featured high in the popularity charts in many countries, notably the UK, the US, South Africa and Australia.

BREED CHARACTERISTICS
Public interest in breeds changes, and it may well be due to today's fast-moving and violent society that a premium is placed on dogs with the ability to act as guards, protectors and watch dogs; hence the popularity of the German Shepherd Dog, Dobermann, Rottweiler etc.

To be all things to all men is a heavy demand to place on a breed. However, to those people who understand and appreciate a highly intelligent dog, with marked guarding instincts, who thrives on human companionship, the Rottweiler fits this description. The breed is special: in its adaptability, its intelligence, and the capacity to form a warm bond with its family. Add to these qualities, boldness, determination, working ability, confidence and strength of will, and you have a dog whose energies and intelligence need to be specifically channelled by the owner.

The owner must understand the Rottweiler, train the dog in manners, and be the pack leader. It is very necessary for the owner to assume this role; if he does not, then the dog will. Physically, the Rottweiler is very powerful, but this does not mean that every Rottweiler needs an owner with the build of a Sumo wrestler! Many small women (including myself) number amongst those who achieve very successful partnerships with members of the breed.

The early days of the Rottweiler: Rott von Berneuchen, born in 1912.

Criticisms of stubbornness and wilfulness have sometimes been levelled, and while Rottweilers *can* be stubborn if an owner adopts a heavy-handed and macho approach, those who utilise the breed's play-loving traits, and make training fun with lots of praise, do not have problems. A physical confrontation between man and dog is counter-productive and quite unnecessary, if the dog has been trained in a kindly way, with lots of praise and play.

As a working dog, the Rottweiler has an excellent nose which makes it an effective tracking and search dog. The Rottweiler is agile and quick to learn, and it possesses sufficient protective instincts which make it unnecessary to 'train' a dog to guard. However, the age at which these instincts are first manifested varies from dog to dog, and it is unrealistic to expect young puppies to guard – although some new owners are disappointed when they do not!

OWNER RESPONSIBILITES

"A Dog is for Life, not just for Christmas" is a slogan well-known to dog lovers. But today's society is a 'throwaway' one, demanding rapid satisfaction, or else replacement of the unsatisfactory object. Dog ownership is changing radically and everywhere there is a marked decline in tolerance towards dogs. Stiff legislation has been introduced to ensure conformity to the public demand for a well-behaved, docile dog, which fits into an increasingly complex society.

This means that anyone who wants to own a dog needs to consider:
1. What breed do you want?
2. Are you suited to own that breed?
3. Do you have the facilities (home environment, time, money) to care for such a dog?

It is vital to take the time and effort to make a short-list of breeds that initially attract, read books on those breeds, and visit owners and kennels. You should then, hopefully, be in a position to make an informed choice so that you and your puppy will be compatible, and your dog will not be destined to become a canine 'discard'.

IS A ROTTWEILER RIGHT FOR YOU?

In recent years, the Rottweiler has attracted much attention, and the breed's popularity has meant that many owners have rushed out to buy a one, without considering the implications of owning a sizable dog of strong character. Dogs measure up to 27 inches at the shoulder, and bitches up to 25 inches; the breed is sturdily built, with weights ranging from about 80-120lbs, although specimens which are outside this range may be found. Not surprisingly, most people view Rottweilers as large, and for their size they are extremely powerful, very active, and require a moderate amount of exercise. Therefore, if you live in a high-rise or small flat it is feasible to own a Rottweiler, but it is not to be recommended!

Just as human beings vary in intelligence, so do breeds of dogs, and on the canine scale, the Rottweiler is a very bright dog indeed. This means that he needs mental stimulation, exercise, close involvement with his family, and some basic training in order to establish a rewarding relationship with his owners. No dog of any breed should be left alone for hours on end, tied up in a yard, or confined to a shed – this constitutes mental cruelty. You should not have any dog, let alone a highly intelligent Rottweiler, if you intend to keep it in this manner.

Involvement with the family is the reason most people want a dog, and Rottweilers make eminently satisfactory companions. They are affectionate, playful and fun-loving; they like to accompany their owners on walks, as well as in the car, and to be with them in the home. Excessive barking is not a complaint that can be levelled at the breed and, while extremely alert watchdogs, they only bark when there is a reason. In the house they are relaxed, and in no way restless.

WILL YOU BE THE PACK LEADER?

All this makes Rottweilers sound paragons amongst dogs – active, intelligent, playful – so why is it emphasised that they are not suitable for all owners? Simply for this reason: like the German Shepherd Dog, Dobermann and other similar breeds, the Rottweiler has well-developed guarding instincts, and owners of such breeds need to understand and channel these instincts by simple basic training in manners. Through

LEFT: The Rottweiler is highly intelligent with marked guarding instincts, who thrives on human companionship.

BELOW: Three 'rescue' dogs who have been successfully rehomed. Think very carefully before taking on the responsibility of owning a dog, especially a big, powerful Rottweiler.

ABOVE: The Rottweiler needs mental stimulation, exercise, and close involvement with his family, plus some basic training.
BELOW: The Rottweiler has a strong character, but as long as he knows his place, and the owner is established as 'pack leader', he makes an excellent family dog.

'unintentional learning', a dog may learn undesirable behaviour, and it is up to the owners to ensure that he does not.

Guarding instincts apart, the Rottweiler has a strong character, which means it is not the right breed for an owner who does not have the will to be dog's pack-leader. A dog that is allowed to dominate the household will assert itself in a number of unpleasant ways, such as possessiveness with objects or food, refusal to obey simple commands, and aggression towards other dogs or people. Not all of us are suited to riding a mettlesome, thoroughbred horse, and in the same way, some people are much more suited to owning one of the gentler breeds. If you intend to own a Rottweiler, you must be responsible for bringing it up to be sufficiently well-behaved so that the dog fits into today's society, and is a pleasant companion to its owners.

The Austrian writer, Adolf Ringer, gives a most apt description of the breed, which highlights the essentials of the Rottweiler's character:

"He does not tolerate being pushed here and there. He has to know where he belongs and then commits himself without qualification. He reacts with defiance and stubbornness to loud shouting and domineering behaviour on the part of his handler or family members. He behaves in a friendly way towards children, but does not put up with being tormented. He .... is a dog of sound character, quiet and calm, and not upset by trifles. Nevertheless he is always watchful and vigilant."

Chapter Two

FINDING A PUPPY

This Chapter has been entitled 'Finding a Rottweiler Puppy', rather than 'Buying', because it is so very easy to go out and buy a puppy; there are many advertisments for them. Whereas, 'finding' a Rottweiler puppy implies a degree of search, and this is exactly what the potential owner should do: seek out the puppy from a litter which looks best suited to their particular needs – and this may well not appear in the first litter seen. All puppies are extremely appealing and difficult to resist, but the head should rule the heart when making this important choice.

LOCATING A BREEDER
There are many advertisments of puppies for sale in the specialist dog papers and magazines, and it is always tempting to go for the breeder that is nearest your home, or the one that has puppies that are instantly ready to go to their new homes. However, it is important to bear in mind that you are taking on a new member of the family who will hopefully live with you for the next decade or more, so it pays to take your time in finding the right breeder.

The national Kennel Club keeps details of all the breed clubs, and if you contact the secretary of one of the clubs, they will be able to put you in touch with some reputable breeders. If you know someone who already owns a Rottweiler, they may also be able to help you.

DOG OR BITCH
Before setting out to view litters, the first decision to make is whether to have a dog or a bitch. It may be that there is already a dog in the household, and so there are specific reasons why you opt for a Rottweiler of the opposite sex, or the same sex. However, there are certain factors which merit careful consideration.

Apart from being larger and stronger, the Rottweiler male has a more forceful and dominant character than the bitch, who rarely wants to be 'leader of the pack.' A male needs an owner who understands canine mentality, who is prepared to undertake training in manners, and who is not soft or weak-willed. If the dog is allowed to follow his own desires, with no discipline instilled into him by his owners, he will grow into an unpleasant, obnoxious animal, who will be a nuisance to all. In an extreme case, this type of dog could end up with a one-way ticket to the veterinarian – a sad and needless waste of life.

The fact that a bitch comes into season about twice a year often deters people from owning one, associating this period with mess, muddle, and hordes of dogs clamouring at the gate. It need be none of these things. Most bitches will keep

Before setting out to view litters you must decide whether you want
dog or a bitch. A male (left) is bigger and heavier and has a mo
dominant nature than a female.

Rottweiler puppies are usually friendly and out-going.

The breeder will ask some searching questions before letting a precious puppy go to a new home.

themselves pretty clean at this time, and the 'danger' time when the bitch is attractive to males is only for a few days of the season, which lasts for a total of approximately twenty-one days. A bitch may be spayed after her first season, or she may be given injections to stop her coming into season. The pros and cons of both methods should be discussed with your vet.

Rottweiler bitches are usually more gentle and affectionate than the males, and they are more amenable in temperament. In fact, many breeders will not sell a male to a first-time owner, suggesting that they start off with a bitch, and go for a male at a later point when they have more experience of the breed.

ASSESSING A LITTER

When you visit a kennel or a breeder's home, make sure that the premises where the puppies are kept are scrupulously clean, and there are no unpleasant smells. It is important to see the mother of the litter, and she should be friendly – not necessarily effusive – but certainly approachable. A nervous or aggressive mother will influence the behaviour of the litter in a negative way, whereas a friendly, out-going bitch will have a beneficial effect on her puppies.

If it is possible, try to see the father of the litter as well, even if it means making a special visit to another kennel. Again, he should be of a friendly and steady disposition. Both parents should have had their hips X-rayed and preferably their eyes and elbows should be checked too. It is not feasible to X-ray puppies of seven to eight weeks as their joints are not fully developed, but if both parents are sound, there is a good chance that they will produce sound stock.

The puppies should be clean, active and friendly, with shining coats and bright eyes. They should not be fat, but just nicely covered. Try not to visit the litter immediately after a meal, for they will tend to be sleepy and lethargic. Rottweiler puppies are usually very out-going little creatures, and while your sympathy may be engaged by a rather retiring, solitary puppy, who appears a little shy, do not select that one. Such a puppy will pose many problems for the new owner.

Regardless of whether puppies are reared in a commercial kennel, or whether they are bred in a private home, it is pivotal to their mental well-being that they have contact with people. This is an aspect of buying a puppy which is sometimes not given sufficient emphasis, but it is crucial. This is where a litter raised in the home can enjoy considerable advantages over puppies reared in a kennel, where it is much harder to provide the stimulation of being with people and experiencing new sights and sounds.

TERMS OF PURCHASE

The breeder should give you as much information as possible about the litter and the parents, and you should also find out whether the litter has been registered with the national Kennel Club (and if not, why not). At the time of purchase, the new owner should be given the registration papers, together with feeding instructions, details of when the puppy was last wormed, and if any inoculations have been given.

Every responsible breeder must be prepared to give an 'after-sales service'; the sale of a puppy does not end at the point where the buyer hands over the purchase price. Breeders should retain a lifelong interest in all their stock, and many ask to be given the chance to re-home the puppy or dog, if the owner has to part with it at any time in the future. If the potential buyer has any doubts at all about the breeder, or does not feel at ease there, then it is better to go elsewhere. Equally, the breeder will be anxious to ensure that their puppies are going to suitable homes, and so you should be prepared to answer some pretty searching questions before the sale goes through. The breeder will want to know about your experience with dogs, the size of your house, whether you have a garden, the size of your family, whether you go out to work, and whether you are willing to attend training classes with your dog. The buyer should not be offended by this, rather the reverse. If the breeder asks *no* questions then the buyer should be very concerned, for it is likely that that the breeder's aims are purely monetary.

A WORD OF WARNING

There is a tendency, particularly with first-time buyers, to think that if they buy two puppies from the same litter, they will be company for each other. Regardless of which sex you choose, this is a mistake. Two puppies demand an enormous investment of time and energy on the part of the owner, and to achieve their full potential, each puppy needs to have daily, individual attention and training, away from its companion. This should be for at least fifteen minutes every day, longer, if possible.

If the puppies are of the same sex, as they reach adolescence there may well be battles to decide which one is dominant. No owner wants to be confronted with the task of trying to separate two young, strong Rottweilers who are intent on having a serious set-to. It is far better to start with one puppy; concentrate on the training so that you have a well-behaved, well-adjusted adult, and *then* acquire a companion, preferably of the opposite sex.

Watch the puppies playing together and you will learn something of their individual characters.

A puppy arriving at his new home will feel bewildered to begin with and will need plenty of reassurance.

Chapter Three

THE EARLY DAYS

PREPARATIONS
The choice is made, dog or bitch; you are satisfied that your breeder has good stock, rears the puppies well and will take an interest in them once they have left for their new homes.

Preparations for the homecoming of your puppy need to be made well in advance of collection, to ensure the smoothest possible transition from nest to new owner. Decide where your puppy is going to sleep, what type of bed to use, and who is going to be responsible for feeding and exercise. It is infinitely preferable that a puppy lives indoors as part of the family. In this way, he quickly becomes accustomed to the ways of the household, so commencing his training in lifemanship!

However, it is an undeniable fact that Rottweiler puppies have strong teeth, and they use them on a whole variety of objects, forbidden or otherwise. If anything 'interesting' is within reach, the puppy will investigate its durability, so before collecting your pup, have a quick look round the house to make sure there are no objects he can grab. If your Rottweiler is subsequently found with a precious shoe or pair of gloves, it is the owner's fault for leaving them in an accessible place!

SLEEPING QUARTERS
There are various types of beds available, such as baskets, plastic beds, beanbags, filled blankets, but for a puppy, with its propensity to chew, it is an unnecessary expense to buy one of these. The very best solution is to have a collapsible indoor kennel or crate, which has a removable 'floor' of plastic or metal. Cover this with layers of newspaper, and on top put a blanket or the fleecy, washable type of bedding.

In the United States crates are widely used, but there is still a feeling among some owners that it is cruel to crate a youngster. However, this method of housing, correctly carried out, has various benefits. It is an easy way of house training the puppy; it gives him a 'den' of his own to retire to, and rest undisturbed; and it provides a way of keeping him secure, to prevent chewing when the owner is not present. Although crates are not cheap, they last a lifetime, and it is advisable to buy a size large enough to accommodate an adult Rottweiler. The crate is collapsible so it can be taken in the car, and used in a hotel bedroom (this is often a stipulation of the management, when the dog is left unattended).

An ordinary cardboard box, without metal staples, is a cheap, easily replaceable alternative bed, which can be used while the puppy is still at the chewing stage, but,

of course, it is not secure. Cover the bottom with newspapers, with a blank
some type of bedding for the top layer. Neither a puppy, nor an adult should
on a bare surface, whether it is wood, tile or cement, and the sleeping area s
be free from draughts. If your Rottweiler is to live in an outdoor kennel, the
building must be waterproof and draughtproof, with a suitable bed.

TOYS

Puppies, all puppies, chew. This happens particularly during teething, when the
teeth are coming out and being replaced by the permanent teeth This sta
about twelve weeks, and during this period, when the gums are sore, it is use
have hard chew toys available which can be kept in a 'toy box'. The safest toy
made of *hard* rubber, available from pet shops in the form of rings, bones et
not disdain aged tough jeans, torn into strips and knotted, which provide lc
entertainment.

Despite the fact that many owners allow their dogs to play with a ball, this m
dangerous because balls can become lodged in the throat, defying efforts to dis
them, with predictably fatal results. If you want your puppy to play with a
ensure that it is made of solid rubber, and that it is too big to lodge in
Rottweiler's throat; it is quite surprising how large this is!

Do not permit the puppy to play with anything wooden because of the dang
splinters. Bones represent many hours of delight to puppies and dogs alike, but
should only be the heavy beef marrow kind that will not splinter. A second pha
chewing is likely to occur at about nine months of age when the permanent
are settling into the gums.

FEEDING AND FEEDING DISHES

Before bringing your puppy home, ask the breeder for a diet sheet to c
development to adulthood, and ensure you have a supply of the food in s
Whether or not you wish to continue with this feeding regime, the diet must or
changed gradually, otherwise the puppy will suffer an upset stomach.

Food and water bowls should be made of stainless steel. Plastic bowls, admit
cheaper, are eminently chewable, and pieces could lodge in your puppy's th
Earthenware bowls tend to crack rather easily. In the case of heavy, rapidly grc
Rottweiler puppies, it is a good idea to have the feeding dish on a stand, so avo
any strain on young, immature muscles and ligaments.

Young children should never be given the responsibility of feeding a puppy
adult, as they quickly become bored with routine chores. Instead, this task mu
the responsibility of an adult member of the household.

COLLECTING YOUR PUPPY

When the great day comes, make sure your puppy is not fed before the journ
avoid the risk of car sickness. If possible, take another adult with you to driv
car, leaving you free to look after the puppy. Some new owners like to have
puppy sitting on their knees on a blanket or towel, while others prefer the pup
be in the back of an estate car, or in a crate. Whatever the method adop
remember that this is the most traumatic experience your puppy will have had
he will need reassurance to deal with the bewildering new world. In case the p
drools or is sick, it is a good idea to take tissues or paper, together with a

plastic bag to use for the rubbish.

When you arrive home, do not let other adults or children overwhelm the puppy. Let the pup explore, keeping you in view all the time, and then an hour or so after arrival, offer something to eat. This should be exactly the same meal as the breeder would have provided. Clean water should always be available, and this should be changed several times a day.

HOUSE TRAINING

Young puppies need to eliminate much more frequently than adults because of their limited bladder capacity. This is especially so during the day, but less so at night when the puppy is sleeping. The golden rules are to take your puppy outside every time he wakes up, after eating or drinking, after playing, and if you see him sniffing the ground and circling.

Select a 'toilet area' in the garden or yard and always take the puppy to that place, using a command such as 'Be quick', and allowing time for the pup to sniff around there. Always praise lavishly when your puppy has performed! At first, he will have absolutely no idea what you mean, but by constantly repeating the same command, he will catch on very quickly.

Never correct a puppy for making a mess in the house, unless you actually catch it in the act. The puppy will not associate the past action with your displeasure. However, if you do come upon the pup transgressing, utter a stern 'Ahhh', and take him outside to the toilet area. In the early days of house training, the watchword is vigilance.

A strategy for house training which is becoming increasingly popular with dog owners, is crate training. Puppies do not like soiling their sleeping quarters, and so the business of house training is accelerated. Initially, when the puppy needs to eliminate frequently, e.g. overnight, it will use one end of the crate, hence the need for a newspaper base, with a blanket at the other end.

A puppy may be upset when first confined to a crate but persevere, for, in time, all puppies get accustomed to this 'den' and will readily go in and stay there, even when the door is left open. A young puppy should never be confined to his crate for long periods – no more than forty-five minutes – except overnight. Put your puppy in his crate for a rest after a meal, after hectic periods of playing, when you are out of the room to ensure chewing of valued objects does not occur, and, of course, at night. Never put your puppy in the crate as a punishment.

One great advantage of a collapsible crate is that it can be taken from room to room, so that your Rottweiler puppy can be with you as much as possible, under controlled circumstances. Apart from the expense of replacing or repairing objects that have been chewed by your puppy, such as furniture, carpets, or shoes, the displeasure it provokes is one of the quickest ways to ruin the developing bond between dog and owner; hence the inestimable value of a crate.

For those people who decide not to buy a crate, house training is accomplished by putting newspapers on the floor, and gradually reducing the area until the papers are right by the door. The puppy should also be taken out regularly, and should never be scolded if you come back and find the pup has made a mess in your absence. Recently, someone mentioned the 'cure' of rubbing the puppy's nose in the mess – I thought that method had gone out with creating a fire by rubbing two sticks together! This way is *wrong* and should never, never be used.

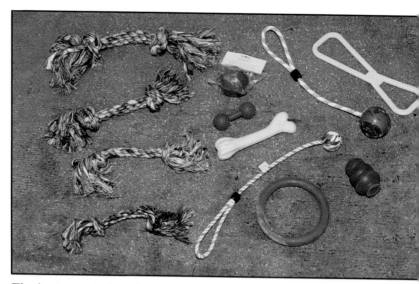

The best toys to buy for your puppy are tough, cotton raggers, which a
virtually indestructible. Other toys should be made of hard rubber, suc
as rings, bones etc.

Food and water bowls should be made of stainless steel. Plastic bowls
are likely to be chewed, and ceramic bowls crack easily.

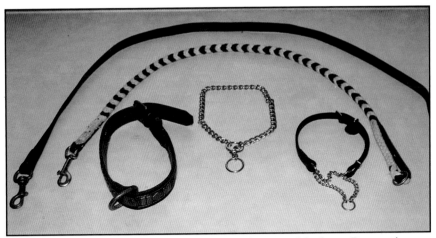

The type of choke chains, collars and leads suiteable for a Rottweiler.

An adult Rottweiler needs a period of free-running exercise every day, but a growing puppy must have limited and controlled exercise.

FOOTNOTE

While puppies are fascinating little creatures, they can also be very trying: w
unsupervised they can get into all sorts of mischief which, for them, is good hea
fun! Their natural inquisitiveness, activity level and propensity to chew, highlight
necessity for the owner to institute a consistent and careful system of training,
the ultimate aim of having a puppy able to fit into his environment, and a plea
to own.

EXERCISE

A young, fast growing, heavy Rottweiler puppy is very vulnerable to stresses
strains, and there are some rules about exercise which the owner should follow:

1 Do not allow your puppy to go up and down stairs. The puppy should
prevented from doing this, or carried.
2. Do not let your puppy climb or jump into or out of cars. He must be lifted in
out.
3. Do not allow your puppy to play with other dogs, either young or old, sma
large, without supervision, and even then only for a very short period. Experie
within the breed has shown that much damage can be done to a puppy if h
allowed to play roughly with an older dog.
4. Do not exercise your puppy during the hottest part of the day in very w
weather. Restrict the puppy's exercise while he is small, and ensure he has plent
rest.

When your puppy is about three months old, you can start off by taking him
200-300 yard walks on the lead, and this distance can be built up gradually. By
time your Rottweiler is ten to twelve months old, you can be doing walks of at
half a mile. *Do not* be tempted to jump your dog until it is at least eighteen mo
old.

Free running exercise is good for a dog, but make sure that the area is suita
such as a field, or a park, or a beach (but not at peak visiting hours!) and y
Rottweiler must be utterly reliable on the recall. People will be frightened at the s
of a large black-and-tan dog hurtling towards them at full tilt!

If your puppy or adult is lame at any time, and the condition persists beyond a
days, you must have him checked by the vet. At the first signs of lameness rest y
dog, only allowing him into the garden on a lead for toiletting purposes. After
operation, instructions concerning exercise given by the vet should be follow
precisely.

Chapter Four

FEEDING

INTRODUCTION

Establishing a good feeding regime is essential to the health and well being of your Rottweiler, and this can best be done by observing some important guidelines:

1. Establish a regime from the outset and always feed in the same place and at the same times.
2. All food should be fed at room temperature; meals should not be served cold, straight from the refrigerator, or hot from a saucepan.
3. Food should be prepared as near to feeding time as possible. If it is prepared too long in advance, changes can take place which may adversely affect the dog.
4. Food should never be kept from one meal to another. Discard any leftovers, as stale food can cause stomach upsets.
5. Do not make sudden changes of diet. New food should be introduced in small quantities.
6. Fresh water should always be available. If the water becomes dirty from saliva or food debris, change it.
7. Never exercise immediately before or after feeding; allow at least one hour either way.
8. In very warm weather, it is inadvisable to feed during the heat of the day.
9. Only give marrow bones, *never* any other kind of bone which can splinter, with dire consequences.
10. A dog's food requirements differ according to age, lifestyle, and state of health.

CHOOSING A DIET

There are various types of dog food on the market: complete diets which contain everything, including all the vitamins and minerals a dog needs, canned meats, and, of course, fresh meat, often prepared in minced form especially for dogs. Whatever kind you decide to feed, remember that large breeds like the Rottweiler have a great deal of growing to do in a very short time, so a balanced diet is essential for health and growth.

Rottweilers are usually very good 'doers'; they enjoy their food and eat with gusto. Like Oliver Twist, they always seem to ask for more! However, it is important not to give too generous a portion, for although a plump puppy may look appealing to the eyes of the uninitiated, excess weight places too much strain on developing muscles and ligaments, and a slightly lean puppy is a much healthier proposition. A 'lean' puppy should be well covered with a waistline, but not 'podgy'.

*LEFT:
Rottweilers
usually enjoy
their food and
eat with gusto!*

*BELOW:
Marrow bones
are good for
your dog's teeth,
but never give
any other type
of bone.*

A dog competing in Working Trials or Agility competitions needs a larger food intake, but this must be in the form of increased calories, not increased protein.

As a dog gets older, the metabolism slows down and fewer calories are required.

DIETARY REQUIREMENTS

New owners should have received a diet sheet from the breeder which should be followed, initially at least, even if it is intended to change to other foods. While exact quantities of food cannot be laid down since each has individual requirements, frequency of feeding is as follows:

Seven weeks to sixteen weeks: four meals daily.
Four months to seven months: three meals daily.
Eight months upwards: two meals daily.
It is better to feed twice a day, morning and evening, as the dog's stomach is not then overloaded by one large meal.

When feeding four meals daily to a young pup, my own diet sheet is:
BREAKFAST and TEA: Puppy meal or cereal such as Farex, or rice, or porridge mixed with milk (full cream), to which a little glucose has been added. Add one egg yolk (*not* egg white) to one of these meals.
LUNCH and SUPPER: Soaked plain puppy meal with either raw or cooked meat. Add vitamin and mineral supplements and sterilised bone flour or bonemeal (which consists of calcium and phosphorus in the correct ratio).

Never exceed the recommended dose for supplements. The idea that 'if a little is good, more is even better' is wrong, and can cause serious problems. Over the years I have given dogs of all ages about half-a-teaspoon cod-liver oil and malt after supper. Pups love licking it from a spoon! If pure cod-liver oil is given, this should be just *one drop* a day.

From four months, when the puppy is on three meals daily, my diet is:
BREAKFAST: Milk meal as before, plus one egg yolk.
LUNCH: Meat meal as before, and supplements.
SUPPER: As for lunch.
As the puppy grows, increase the amounts at all meals.

When the Rottweiler is on two meals, I would feed:
BREAKFAST: Milk and egg yolk as before.
SUPPER Meat as before, and supplements.
Increase quantities.
Note: Supplements should be given once a day only (with one meal).

Some puppies decide at quite an early age that they do not want milk any more. This can be replaced with solid biscuits to chew – small ones initially – varied occasionally by giving rice, or porridge, or cereal. By the time the puppy is twelve months old, you should aim to be feeding an all-carbohydrate (biscuits) breakfast, and an all-meat (plus supplements) supper. I believe this aids digestion and is desirable in large, deep-bodied breeds in which a serious condition known as 'bloat' and 'gastric torsion' sometimes occurs (see Chapter 8).

Puppies and adults differ greatly in their food requirements, and it is not possible to specify exact amounts. At seven weeks, start at about 6-8 ozs meat (3-4 ozs lunch and supper), and aim for the ration to contain 60 per cent carbohydrate and 40 per cent meat. Thinking has changed over the years and it is now recommended that dogs are fed less meat and more carbohydrate. As the puppy grows these amounts must be increased, but decreased when maximum growth is reached.

TIDBITS
Apart from their use as a reward when training, some owners find it pleasurable to give their Rottweilers tidbits between meals – and the dogs certainly approve! It is important to bear two points in mind: first, it is an unkindness to allow a dog to become fat (it is the well-covered dog, not the plump animal which is the healthier), and second, do not allow the dog to solicit tidbits by whining, barking, drooling or looking pathetic! Let your dog earn its reward by sitting on command, carrying a small object, or in some other way gaining your approval.

SPECIAL NEEDS
Careful attention must be paid to your Rottweiler's dietary needs at all stages of life. What is called a 'maintenance diet' may be fed after the age of twelve to fourteen months'; this is the amount of food the average companion dog needs to keep fit and healthy.

Working dogs such as police dogs or, to a lesser extent, dogs which compete in Working Trials, Obedience or Agility competitions require more food. This is an increase in calories, not protein. High protein diets can be positively dangerous to health.

The aging dog usually lives a more sedentary life and does not require so many calories. However, the veteran will need more calcium in order to maintain the skeleton (in the form of bonemeal or bone flour), but not so much fat, as this is difficult for the older dog to digest. Consistency of eating habits is extremely important at this stage of a dog's life, and at least two meals a day should be given.

Whelping and rearing a litter places great demands on a bitch, and this is a stressful time. She must be fed increased amounts more frequently. Remember that her health and general condition have a profound effect on the future health of the puppies.

THE SICK DOG
Illnesses, such as kidney failure, digestive or absorption problems, diabetes mellitus, obesity, heart disease etc., dictate a special regime of feeding, and the owner must scrupulously follow the advice of the veterinarian.

FOOD ALLERGIES/DEFICIENCIES
Dogs may be allergic to certain foodstuffs, e.g. milk, beef or beef by-products, eggs, fish, to mention a few, just as there can be a deficiency of some mineral, vitamin or enzyme, giving cause for concern through signs like skin disease, digestive upsets and failure to put on condition. Such problems need careful investigation, and the advice of a veterinarian or clinician is essential.

With proper training, the Rottweiler will behave well in a busy urban environment. This Rottweiler lives in New York.

Chapter Five

SOCIALISATION AND TRAINING

INTRODUCTION

Socialisation is the term used for introducing a puppy sensibly, safely and non-traumatically to all the situations it is likely to meet in his life. This involves meeting people, other animals, encountering different objects, sights, sounds and smells, enabling the dog to fit into adult life, adapting to its demands and constraints in a way which is acceptable to society, and which gives pleasure and satisfaction to the owner.

It is impossible to over-estimate the importance of socialisation, and its influence on the mental development of any dog. It brings out a dog's full potential, and in large breeds of strong character, such as Rottweilers, German Shepherd Dogs and Dobermanns, training and socialisation should start from the time the puppy first arrives home. In order to facilitate this adaptation to life through the twin routes of socialisation and training, it is necessary to understand the developmental stages that all puppies go through, so that the owner may deal with situations as they arise.

STAGES OF DEVELOPMENT

CANINE SOCIALISATION

By the time the puppy arrives at its new home at the age of seven to eight weeks, it will have reached the Canine Socialisation Stage (29-49 days). Prior to this, the puppy will have 'learned to become a dog' by interacting with its littermates, learning body language and different vocalisations. Discipline is taught by the mother.

A word of warning here: *never* take a puppy from a breeder when it is younger than seven weeks of age. Such puppies tend to be noisier and more prone to fighting, and they never reach their full potential. Any assurances to the contrary which a breeder may give are without foundation!

HUMAN SOCIALISATION

This stage occurs between seven to twelve weeks (50-84 days), and this is when you should take the time and trouble to begin training, which *must be non-punitive*. Of course, puppies should have met people from the age of three to four weeks. Learning at this time is permanent and rapid, and the puppy can be taught all the commands he will need to know. Formation of attachments, 'bonding' as it is termed, is at its peak at eight weeks of age, therefore it is important to create a kind and sympathetic environment for the puppy.

The puppy cannot be taken out on roads and areas frequented by other dogs the course of inoculations is complete, but you can take him out in the car, into town and country (to see other animals). Hold the puppy in your arms, not put him down on the pavement, and in this way he will become accustomed to the n of streets, awash with people and traffic. Do not allow well-intentioned people swoop down on your puppy, only permit carefully introduced gentle petting.

At this time, puppies will bite in play, and you must teach bite inhibition. W your puppy nips, say "Ouch" in a sharp tone, which is usually sufficient to stop biting. If it is not, then take the puppy by the scruff of the neck, shake, and gi light slap on the nose. Discipline is instant and over, as it would be given by mother in the nest.

FEAR IMPACT
This period occurs between 56-77 days, and this is when any traumatic physica mental experiences have a lasting effect. So when you take your puppy for inoculations, give him a big hug when the needle goes in, as touch masks learn Ask the veterinarian to pet your puppy when it is all over, and give a tidbit. Bev of punitive house-training; the puppy can develop a fear of the person who gr him. This is a time to 'cushion' your puppy against anything unpleasant frightening.

SENIORITY CLASSIFICATION
This stage occurs between twelve to sixteen weeks of age when the puppy start 'cut the apron strings' and may test for dominance. (Note: not all Rottweilers w to become the pack leader, but it is as well to know the signs.) Play biting mouthing must be firmly discouraged, so should biting of the lead, since thi regarded by the puppy as an extension of the owner's arm. There should be games involving shows of strength, wrestling, tugs-of-war etc. Men usually insti these!

THE FLIGHT INSTINCT
This period is of variable duration. It occurs between four and eight months corresponds to physical adolescence. The dog begins to explore the environm and stops coming when called. Training, which should have begun earlier, takes c of this problem.

FEAR OF NEW SITUATIONS
This is usually related to growth spurts, and occurs between approximately six fourteen months of age. Dogs will suddenly show fear of something familiar. Do force any dog to confront the thing which frightens him. Handle the situation remaining calm and ignoring your dog's reaction. Try to 'jolly' your dog through fears; do not adopt a 'macho' approach, or use soothing talk. The best course action is to continue socialisation and training.

YOUNG ADULTHOOD AND MATURITY
This is the final stage of development, and can occur from twelve months to fi years; the larger the breed, the later it is. This period is characterised by the incre in size and strength, mental as well as physical. A very dominant dog (and there

not so many of these) may renew the test for leadership. This type of dog should be treated firmly and kindly, while continuing with training.

MAN/DOG RELATIONSHIP
These critical periods have been dealt with in some detail because it is so important to the permanence and satisfaction of the man/dog relationship that the owner understands the way a dog develops. With this knowledge the owner can use the tools of training and socialisation to deal with any problems that arise. Start training in a happy, encouraging way from Day One, bearing in mind the following points:
1. A young puppy's powers of concentration are very limited, so keep training periods short (5-10 minutes maximum).
2. Be consistent in the words you use when you are giving commands.
3. Tell the puppy once only what to do, as soon he has learnt the command.
4. Give rewards in the form of tidbits and/or praise.
5. Have regular play periods with both puppies and adult dogs.

To sum up: there are five ways of rewarding the puppy (the Five Ps – from Roy Hunter, *Anglo-American Dog Training*):
PRAISE, PET, POP (tidbit), PLAY, PLEASANT EXPRESSION AND BODY POSTURE.
To own a well-mannered, pleasant, happy dog demands some time and effort – on the part of the owner.

TRAINING YOUR ROTTWEILER
I have emphasised that all dogs need some form of training to enable them to fit into society and life generally, otherwise problems will arise, usually resulting in the dog being passed on to another person or put down. A Rottweiler grows very rapidly into a large, powerful dog, with a high activity level and a strong character, so it would be very foolish for any owner to postpone giving simple manners training 'until the puppy is a bit older'. It is one thing to teach a young puppy to sit, lie down, and obey other basic commands, but quite another to deal with a 100lbs dog who does not feel particularly co-operative.

BASIC MANNERS
The time to start showing your Rottweiler what is required, is from the time he first arrives home. Your puppy needs to learn:

1. To come when called ("Come").
2. To sit or lie down ("Sit, "Drop").
3. To stay ("Stay", "Wait").
4. To give up objects, including bones, when told ("Leave" or "Give").
5. Not to pull when out on a lead ("Heel").

Allow your puppy a couple of days or so to settle and find his way round, for moving to a new home is very unsettling, and decide what words you are going to use for specific commands. *Always* keep to the same commands otherwise the puppy will be totally confused. Make sure the whole family know what these commands are. Never nag the puppy; it has a depressing effect on him.

A well-sociali...
Rottweiler wi...
take every ne...
situation in h...
stride, and
getting on an...
off a bus
presents no
problems for
this dog.

This Rottweiler
is perfectly
calm, sitting
alongside a
noisy steam
train.

The ultimate test – a busy airport with planes taking off and landing – and this Rottweiler passes with flying colours.

Crates have enormous advantages when training your Rottweiler – not least when you are travelling by car.

CRATE TRAINING

Crate training should begin immediately, so have the crate ready with a paper layer covered by a blanket, and let the puppy investigate it. Settle on the command you intend to use, such as "Crate", or "Bed", and keep to it. Give the command, lift the puppy straight in and out, praise lavishly and give a tidbit. Build up time gradually and then close the crate door, but take the puppy straight out again.

Next, try to coax the puppy to go in, using a tidbit as an incentive *when* he is inside, as well as giving lots of praise. Gradually build up the time your puppy is in the crate, starting to leave him alone in it for a few minutes while you leave the room. Sometimes a puppy is apprehensive of the crate, in which case feed the puppy alongside the crate, and then bring the food bowl closer until eventually you are feeding the pup inside the crate. *Never* use the crate as punishment, and never leave the puppy in it for long periods – forty-five minutes as a maximum during daylight hours, and five to six hours overnight.

When teaching your puppy any of the following exercises, initially try to do it in a distraction-free environment like a quiet corner of the garden or an empty room, otherwise people moving about, noises, cooking smells and so on will interfere with the pup's concentration. As learning progresses and your Rottweiler matures, distractions can and should be introduced.

All training of young puppies must be kind, sympathetic and consistent. Patience is vital. Puppies are very ready to learn, inquisitive and receptive to the right approach, but it must be remembered that their span of concentration is not that of an adult dog. Now is the time to lay the foundations for a happy, well-trained and well-adjusted dog who can be a marvellous 'accessory' to your life.

COMING WHEN CALLED

It is important to remember that the dog is a pack animal, and two or more together can behave in a different, less disciplined way, however well trained they are. Particular care should be taken to ensure that control can be maintained when more than one dog is allowed off the lead at a time. Do not assume you have that control, test it first in a controlled environment. This is absolutely vital.

Use a simple command like "Come", which has a staccato ring to it. Always use a light happy tone of voice, and always make a puppy or adult feel wanted when he comes to you. Crouch down to the level of the puppy when calling, giving lots of praise and, if you wish, a tidbit on arrival. I use dog 'choc drops' or hard biscuit, both of these broken into very small pieces. Give rewards (praise, tidbits) immediately, otherwise your puppy will not associate the reward with the action. Never disdain the use of food in training; its use accelerates learning.

A puppy must always associate coming to the owner with pleasure, and no matter what heinous crime has been committed (in the owner's eyes), the pup must *never* be punished when he comes. If this happens, in future the puppy will come with reluctance and suspicion, if at all, and this will be to the detriment of the relationship. It is important to teach your puppy to come when called, before he has learned to run away.

THE 'SIT'

Your puppy naturally knows how to sit, so it is a question of his doing this every time you ask. To teach this, use a tidbit; hold it a little in front of the pup, slightly higher than eye level, then move your hand towards you and say "Sit". Looking at the tidbit causes the puppy to sit, whereupon he is given the reward and praised with a "Good dog".

A puppy does not always sit, so repeat the command, and with your other hand press gently on his back just above the tail, then give the tidbit. Practise this every day for about a week, with four to six repetitions at a time, then try to get your puppy to obey with command only; and then give the reward. Eventually give the tidbit only every second or third time. Remember that puppies have delicate bones and joints, so do not be clumsy in your handling.

If food does not work, try the following method. Position your puppy, standing by your left side. Place your right hand in front of the pup's chest, and gently slide your left hand down his back, tucking the puppy into a sit by applying pressure equally behind stifles and against chest.

TO 'LIE DOWN'
This is an exercise to teach the dog to remain in the same position for some time, e.g. if you are having a meal, writing or have visitors. Again, dogs know naturally how to lie down, and it is a matter of teaching your puppy to respond to the command. To teach the command, get your puppy sitting by your left side (this is the side always used in Obedience training circles). With your left hand hold the collar, and in your other hand have a tidbit. Show your puppy the tidbit, then lower it straight down to the floor in front of the puppy. At the same time, press gently downwards on the collar and give the command you intend to use, "Down", "Drop", or "Flat". When your puppy lies down, praise and give the tidbit.

Practise this as for the sit (above) over several days until the puppy will lie down immediately, then use pressure on the collar only and finally command only.

TO 'STAY'
The stay exercise has many very practical applications, and once the pup knows the exercises above, he can be taught to stay in one place for increasing lengths of time.

The exercise can be started by having your puppy sit by a door and allowed to go through, after about fifteen seconds, when the owner says "OK" or "Right". You can also get your puppy to sit and wait a few seconds before being given his food, before getting into or out of a car, at a roadside kerb, and before being petted. Do not permit the puppy to decide to get up when he wants, you must give the release command "OK". If your puppy moves, then put him back in the sit position. Your puppy should not be expected to remain in the sit position for more than a minute.

It is not advisable to try to teach the 'Stay' first thing in the morning, after the puppy has been asleep, or in his crate, as he will be feeling very 'bouncy' and disinclined to keep still. Once the puppy lies down on command, select a place and give the command "Stay". (It is helpful for the owner to have a chair or stool to sit on!) If the puppy attempts to get up, put him down again, and repeat the exercise until he stays.

To begin with, have the puppy stay for a minute, praise and release with an "OK". Practise and increase the time slowly, remembering only to allow the puppy to get up when you give the release command. With a very lively and active puppy, you can use a lead to prevent him dashing off. If your puppy moves, *always* go back to him, *never* call him to you.

Top breeder and handler Liz Dunhill trains a puppy for the show ring. It is essential to start all training when the puppy is still young. Do not delay until you have a powerful dog on your hands, with a mind of his own.

Teaching your dog the 'Down' command will prove useful in a variety of situations.

With practice, your Rottweiler will be so secure in the 'Stay' that he will be trustworthy, regardless of other distractions.

When teaching your Rottweiler to walk to heel, the aim is to achieve a nice steady pace, controlled by the handler – not by the dog.

COLLAR/LEAD TRAINING

Accustom your puppy to a collar (with name/address tag) when he first arrives home. There are various types of collars available, and for daily wear a leather one with a buckle is recommended. *Never* leave a choke chain on, be it metal, leather or webbing, as this can become caught up and the dog will choke to death. This is not fiction, it is fact, and it has happened to Rottweilers.

For training, use an adjustable collar and ensure that it fits right up behind the ears. Use a webbing or narrow leather lead, 5/6 feet long. Do not use a chain or half-chain lead as these are painful to hold. After the puppy has become familiar with the collar, attach the lead, and allow him to walk around in the home environment, with the lead dragging along. This should be done only under supervision as the lead might become entangled.

When the puppy accepts this, you should take up the end of the lead, and just follow him around. Next, introduce directional control, first offering tidbits to get the puppy to follow, then using the lead for guidance. To introduce walking on the lead and to stop the puppy from pulling, which is most exhausting and irritating for the owner, seek a distraction-free area and position your puppy on your left. Give a command such as "Heel", and start to walk in a large circle. If the puppy pulls ahead, stand still, and guide him back to your side. Repeat the command "Heel", giving a tidbit when the puppy returns to your side. Start with small goals in mind – just a few steps without the puppy pulling – then gradually increase the distance.

STRESS LEVELS

These days we often hear about people suffering from stress, but animals can also suffer from this condition, although it is rarely recognised in dogs. Stress levels range from tolerable to intolerable (resulting in inability to function), and during this time the ability to learn is affected. Indeed, it may cease altogether, so pain and fear should never be introduced during training.

Signs of stress may be increased activity (jumping up, leaping around) or decreased activity (sleepiness, excessive panting, drooling). If a dog is pushed beyond the stress threshold, neurosis develops. This can cause problems in rescue dogs, which means that they may have built-in limitations.

While it is unfortunately true that Rottweilers are sometimes acquired by people who wish to enhance a would-be 'macho' image with a large, aggressive dog, most owners want to have a pleasing companion who fits in well with family life and can be taken about with them on country walks, into towns and on holidays. In short, they want a reliable, well-trained dog. This needs time, effort, patience and kindness, and if you are not prepared to take the trouble to mould your Rottweiler into the kind of dog described, then do not have one.

Chapter Six

UNDESIRABLE BEHAVIOUR

Despite training, sometimes problems do develop, and these need to be identified quickly so that measures to cure them may be started. In my experience, I have found the most common problems are the dog who will not come when called, excessive barking, destructive behaviour, and aggression towards other dogs, and/or people.

NOT COMING WHEN CALLED

Coming when called is a 'must', and if the foundations are well laid (see Chapter Five), then this problem should not arise. However, if it does occur then the owner must go back to basics. Put your puppy/dog on a long line (about 12 feet) and practise calling him to you: "Rover, Come" (one command only), and give a quick tug on line. Reward him with a tidbit and lots of praise. Practise this again and again, in different places with different distractions.

When the dog is reliable, the next step is to leave the line trailing, but make sure you are in a position to take hold of the end of the line before you call your dog, so he cannot make a mistake! Do not be in a hurry to take the line off, wait until you consider your dog is dependable. The next step is to take your Rottweiler to an enclosed area, where he cannot run away, remove the line and, after a few minutes, call your dog to you (one command). If your dog comes, praise and reward; if not, go back to using the line. Do not expect success overnight!

When you are out on a walk with your Rottweiler off-lead, a pitfall to avoid is calling him to you near the end of the walk to put him back on the lead. A dog will soon become wise to this, and will very likely show increasing reluctance to come. Instead, call your dog to you several times during the walk, without putting him on the lead, and praise before letting him run freely again. This means the dog will not form the association: lead, end of walk, won't come.

EXCESSIVE BARKING, CHEWING, DIGGING

While barking is a very natural activity for a dog, Rottweiler owners are fortunate in that the breed is not given to barking without good reason. They are not 'yappers', so this problem does not arise very often. Nevertheless, if a dog is left for hours on end at home while the owners work full time, then barking will occur, so a dog should not be kept under these conditions.

Puppies may sometimes dig, although I have not found Rottweiler puppies do this very often, but they can be great chewers. While teething, puppies need to chew, but there is an underlying cause in the case of an adult who does this. Whichever of

LEFT: Rottweilers must be trained to behave with other dogs, and an owner must ensure that the habit of aggression does not become established.

BELOW: The Rottweiler must be trained so that all the best qualities of his temperament come to the fore.

RIGHT: A head collar (or Halti) is an invaluable training aid to use with large, strong dogs.

BELOW: A rescued Rottweiler, successfully re-homed on a farm, is now a self-appointed guardian of the sheep.

these objectionable behaviours a Rottweiler exhibits, there are some factors which are common to each one: lack of sufficient exercise, isolation and lack of mental stimulation. A dog may also chew in order to attract the owner's attention.

Despite the fact that a Rottweiler does not require as much exercise as some other large breeds, you are inviting problems if you confine him to a flat or a small backyard without giving him a chance for sufficient exercise. Dogs are social creatures; they enjoy the company of their own kind and of humans, so lengthy periods spent on their own can cause what is known as 'separation anxiety'. This results in unwanted behaviour, such as excessive barking, chewing and digging.

This type of anxiety may be triggered off by the owner making a great fuss of the dog when leaving the house. The dog, in a mood of excitement, is left alone and chews, barks or demolishes! To avoid generating this sort of excitement, on leaving or returning to the house, the owner should treat the dog in a calm, almost perfunctory manner, in order that the dog accepts comings and goings as a matter of course. The same applies when leaving the dog in a car.

A highly intelligent dog, like a Rottweiler, needs not only companionship, but enough companionship and interesting, stimulating things to do to prevent boredom, which causes undesirable behaviour. Not all owners play with their dogs, and by play I do not mean 'rough-housing'. This type of 'play' is not a good idea at all; it arouses prey instincts and may encourage the dog to become too boisterous. Never forget that when full grown, the Rottweiler is a very strong dog indeed, so that amount of power hurtling at you at ten or more miles an hour can cause quite a lot of damage!

Games owner and dog may play together include retrieving objects, finding hidden objects, seeking the (hidden) owner or a friend, carrying things like the daily newspaper or a suitable shopping basket. Do not forget that playing games gives your dog an interest, and increases the bond between you.

AGGRESSION TOWARDS OTHER DOGS
Some Rottweilers, usually males, can be aggressive towards other dogs of any breed and size. This is an unpleasant habit which needs checking when first manifested. It is far from uncommon to see owners smiling indulgently while their puppy squares up to another dog, often much larger, growling and with hackles raised. Such behaviour is not so amusing when that puppy becomes a strong adult. It is dangerous and should be stopped at the outset. An owner must be prepared to be very firm with a puppy or an adult to ensure that the habit of aggression does not become established.

Many training clubs now run classes for puppies, so that the pups can get used to other people and other dogs, and the puppies can all play together off lead. However, training classes are not the solution for a dog who has become aggressive towards other dogs, unless the dog is initially handled on his own away from other dogs. This should continue on a one-to-one basis, until the instructor considers the dog is ready to be introduced gradually to the class situation. An experienced trainer is required to deal with this problem.

A check chain or check collar should be worn for training, and when dealing with aggression towards other dogs, it is best to be positive, keeping your voice calm and giving the dog an alternative exercise to do, such as sitting. Get your dog to stay in that position on a short but loose lead, and if the dog attempts to move, re-position him in the sit until the other dog has passed. The owner needs to be vigilant, and at the first sign of hostility, take steps to control the dog before an aggressive situation escalates. A change in behaviour does not happen overnight, and it is stressed that it is far easier to stop the habit developing in a puppy than curing an aggressive adult.

If little or no improvement occurs, then the owner should consult a veterinarian to discuss the advisability of castration.

AGGRESSION TOWARDS PEOPLE

All dogs can bite. Biting most commonly occurs during early adolescence (6-8 months), when the dog reaches maturity (2-3 years), and during its twilight years. The situations which elicit this response include: "being approached, handled, grabbed, or restrained, especially by strangers or visitors; when frightened, hurt, or shy; when protecting food, bones, toys, sleeping areas, cars, houses, yards, offspring and owners; when aggressive and when playful or over-exuberant". (Dunbar and Bonnenkamp, 1985).

The owner should be aware of these situations when trouble may arise, be able to understand and 'read' the dog, and to maintain control through basic manners training, and careful continuous socialisation. Dogs have dignity which strangers must respect, and it is frequently necessary to restrict well-intentioned people who overwhelm the dog with over-enthusiastic, even rough petting. Some people, especially children, have very 'heavy' hands, which the dog may resent.

DOMINANCE

In the dog's eyes, within every household there is a pack leader, who may be two- or four-legged, and it is up to the owner to ensure that this role resides with the human element, otherwise an unsatisfactory and unpleasant situation will result.

Dominant dogs do not suddenly become so. Assumption of a superior position in the household is a slow process; it occurs when a dog of strong character is allowed, through the family's ignorance, to take over as pack leader. This happens in various ways: the dog may be allowed to sleep on the bed, sofa or chair, and then refuse to get down when told; the dog may demand to have his food first, before the family have theirs; he may go through doorways first; demand (and receive) attention whenever he solicits it; he may become possessive with food and objects.

All these privileges belong to a pack leader, and by allowing a dog to behave in this way, the owner is confirming the dog's superiority. To deal with a Rottweiler puppy of strong character, who seems likely to grow into a potentially dominant adult, the owner must ensure that discipline is maintained from the start in a kindly, but firm way. The puppy should not be allowed to persist in any of the unwanted behaviours mentioned above.

Stop your puppy going through doorways first by physically holding him back in the beginning, always giving a command like "Back", progressing to an arm held in front of the pup's chest, then the command only. Do not feed your puppy in isolation, give the pup his food in the kitchen where other activity is taking place, and when another person is present. Get your puppy in the habit of 'earning' his food by sitting first of all – but only for a second.

Food is a very sensitive area, and neither puppy, nor adult should ever be teased or interfered with when feeding. A good idea is for the owner to go to the bowl to drop a little more food in it, thus showing that the proximity of a person is not

In order to prevent possessiveness over food, the owner should drop an extra morsel into the bowl while the dog is feeding, showing that human 'interference' is not threatening

The dog should be trained to look into the owner's eyes on the command "Watch me". This teaches the dog that eye contact is not unsettling, and should not provoke an aggressive response.

A Rottweiler is highly intelligent and must be given tasks to channel his mental energies. This Rottweiler gives regular demonstrations to show off her skills as a goose-herder.

The well-trained, well-socialised Rottweiler will take all situations in his stride, and he will feel no need to prove himself by reacting aggressively.

threatening. If the puppy/adult does become possessive about food, there are a number of things the owner can do, such as hand feed, a mouthful at a time; put successive morsels in the bowl, adding one as the previous one is eaten; or hold the bowl while the dog is feeding.

Dogs may also become possessive over objects, and to avoid this, introduce the 'toys' in a play context, with the owner always initiating the play, and taking away the object at the end of the session. Encourage the puppy or adult to come to you with the object, and give a tidbit and lavish praise when he gives it to you.

BEING HANDLED

From the time the puppy first arrives home, he should become accustomed to being handled. Examine his ears, inspect his teeth, pick up his feet, and clip (or file) his nails, as necessary. The owner should gently stroke/or pat the puppy on his head, neck, shoulders and back, as this prepares the dog for the attention of others, including the veterinarian.

Some dogs find a person staring at them unsettling or threatening, and this may provoke an aggressive response. It is, therefore, recommended that the owner accustoms the puppy to being looked at by holding the pup's head steady, looking into his eyes, and giving lots of praise. Do not keep the young puppy in this position for more than a second, building up to not more than a minute when the dog is adult. Never allow anyone to tease the dog when carrying out this exercise, and a command such as "Watch me" should be introduced to replace the head being held. If the puppy objects to being handled, praise and give a tidbit by way of encouragement when you touch him.

There is as much character variation in dogs as in people, and just as there are potentially dominant dogs, there are also more diffident types who need to be handled gently, and with much encouragement, to equip them for life. No two puppies are alike in temperament. Some puppies are sensitive to noise, and loud commands are demoralising to them, while others are what is called body-sensitive, upset by pressure on the collar or choke chain, or by rough pats. An understanding of individual character is essential if the owner is to bring out the best in the dog, and to establish a rewarding bond.

TRAINING CLASSES

It is well worth while to take your Rottweiler to a training class as soon as the inoculation programme has been completed. Many clubs now run puppy classes, which are an invaluable way of socialising a dog with its own kind. Unfortunately, meeting dogs in the park, or when out for walks is not the best way to do this, as a high proportion are not under the control of their owners, and too many encounters with aggressive dogs are very likely to elicit an aggressive response from your own dog. A puppy class provides the opportunity for your puppy to interact in a friendly way with puppies of different breeds, under controlled circumstances, providing an invaluable learning experience.

Owners should be perfectly clear as to the function of a training class: it is not to train your puppy/dog, it is to advise you how to do this. The greatest care must be taken in the choice of a training class as the quality of instruction varies considerably. Visit several on your own, without taking your Rottweiler, before deciding which to choose. Talk to the secretary or instructor and find out what classes are held. Sit in on a class and observe. Is it crowded with dogs? Is it noisy? Does the instructor shout loudly or handle the dogs roughly? If the answer to some or all of these questions is 'yes', then go elsewhere.

Ideally, a club should run classes for both puppies and adult dogs, varying in duration from six to ten weeks, attendance in each course depending on age, and/or the level of training the dog has reached. Owners generally find these classes fun. It is rewarding to see how the dog progresses, to discuss mutual training problems with other owners, and to graduate with a certificate of proficiency at the end of a course. The time spent attending training classes at a good club represents a valuable investment in your dog's future.

Chapter Seven

THE BREED STANDARD

It may well be that you have no desire to show the family Rottweiler, but the wish to 'have a good one' is often expressed. This means that the dog should adhere closely to the standard for the breed laid down by a country's Kennel Club, both in appearance and temperament. It is, if you like, a 'blueprint' for the breed. The form of words used to describe a Rottweiler varies between countries, but a Rottweiler is a Rottweiler is a Rottweiler, and is recognisable the world over.

INTERPRETING THE STANDARD
Although height and body proportions are laid down, a dog is not just a set of mathematical measures by which he should be judged. Everyone will make an individual interpretation of how any dog fits the standard, and this accounts for the fact that the same dogs do not always win at dog shows!

The female (left) should show distinctly pretty, feminine features; the male (right) has a broader skull and muzzle.

Anatomy of the Rottweiler

1. Muzzle
2. Stop
3. Occiput
4. Withers
5. Back
6. Croup
7. Tail
8. Hock
9. Stifle
10. Tuck up
11. Chest
12. Pastern

GENERAL APPEARANCE

The Rottweiler is a robust sturdy dog, above average in size, not coarse, and certainly not fat. As a working breed he should look as if he has the stamina, musculature and body construction to do a job. There is a marked difference in appearance between dogs and bitches. The male is larger and more powerful in body, with a head broader in skull and muzzle. The bitch is still sturdily built, but is smaller and should have an unmistakably pretty, feminine head. It is a serious fault to have a lightly built dog which looks like a bitch or a heavy bitch with a coarse head that looks like a dog.

The height at the shoulder for dogs is: UK 25in-27in (63-69 cm), USA 24in-27in (61-69 cm); bitches: UK 23in-25in (58-63.5 cm), USA 22in-25in (56-63.5 cm). The ratio of the height at the shoulder to the length of the body (chest to point of buttock) is as 9 to 10, in other words the Rottweiler is slightly longer than tall.

The mature Rottweiler should be balanced, which means that the proportions of the parts of the dog, e.g. height: length of body, depth of brisket: length of forelegs, length of skull: length of muzzle (should be 3 to 2) are in accordance with the breed standard. Weights for dogs and bitches are not mentioned in the standard, but these should be in proportion to the animal's individual build. My own dogs have weighed between 100-115lb, and bitches 80-90lb, but animals exist which are outside these ranges.

Size can, and often does arouse strong feelings, but whether you like a larger or a smaller Rottweiler, the requirements of the Standard must be paramount. A dog that is too large may be clumsy and lack speed and agility, which a working dog should certainly have.

TEMPERAMENT

I have referred many times to the importance of a sound temperament in this book. Both sexes possess a strong character. The breed is extremely intelligent with good guarding instincts, and is very trainable in the right hands. In the wrong hands, the Rottweiler can get into trouble. Many owners do not 'read' their dogs; they have scarcely any knowledge of canine psychology or maybe none at all, and yet they expect their dogs to behave in a socially acceptable way, with little or no human guidance.

Given care and understanding, the Rottweiler exhibits all the qualities you could want in a dog: loyalty, willingness to please, affection and playfulness.

THE HEAD

The head shows much nobility. The skull is broad and flat between the ears, and when a Rottweiler is alert the ears are raised, giving an even broader appearance to the skull. The muzzle is fairly short, broad and deep, and the whole head should be what we term 'dry', meaning that there should be no excess skin in the form of folds or wrinkles on the skull, or on the throat (dewlap), and the lips should be tight and not droopy.

Eyes are an important feature in any dog. In the Rottweiler they should be dark-brown, almond-shaped, and very expressive. They should not be round or light in colour.

Ears are medium-sized and pendant, lying flat and close to the head. Sometimes while teething is taking place, they are folded back and it may be necessary to seek advice from the breeder about massaging or taping these back to put them in the correct position for just a few weeks.

The way in which the ears are held makes a great difference to the appearance of the head. When set on the head correctly they give the impression of greater width to the skull, whereas flying (folded) ears look most untidy and unattractive.That is why advice from the breeder should be sought immediately if the puppy's ears start to fold.

Pigment – nose, eye-rims, lips and gums should be black, but pink mouths and lips are occasionally found. This fault is viewed as serious in some countries, although it certainly has no harmful effect on the dog. It is purely a cosmetic fault, and when viewing a litter of eight weeks it is not possible to say which puppies are likely to have incorrectly pigmented mouths, as pigment changes can occur throughout the life of a dog.

TEETH
A mature dog should have a full complement of teeth (42) and a scissor bite i.e. when the mouth is closed the front teeth (incisors) of the upper jaw fit tightly in front of those of the lower jaw.

COAT AND COLOUR
In the very early days of the breed, colours other than black-and-tan were permitted. The first breed book published in Germany in 1914 mentions dogs which are: "yellow with dark mask and ears, coffee brown with red markings, red without markings".

Nowadays, however, black-and-tan is the only colour recognised. Tan markings, whatever the breed (and in cross-breeds) always appear on the same areas of the body – above each eye, muzzle, legs, chest, and under the tail, varying only in extent and depth of colour. Markings that are too profuse – on the chest, coming up too high on the muzzle and legs – or light, straw-coloured markings are a fault. The desired shade is a deep, rich rust or mahogany. In contrast, some dogs exhibit a condition known as melanism, which is an almost complete absence of markings, and this is also a fault.

The black outer coat is of medium length, coarse in texture and without wave. In healthy animals this has a pleasing gloss. The undercoat may be grey, black or fawn and should not show through the outer coat, although this may happen when a dog is shedding his coat. Sometimes long or excessively wavy coats are seen, and both are faulted in the show ring. Very young puppies have soft almost 'powder-puff' coats which they quickly lose, so that by the time they go to their new homes at seven to eight weeks of age they are wearing sleek jackets! Any pups which have tufts of hair on the ears or much longer hair on the backs of their legs will not develop correct coats.

BODY CONFORMATION
When mature the Rottweiler is a substantial animal with a broad deep chest, reaching to the elbows (not more than, and not much less than 50 per cent of shoulder height), with plenty of room for the vital organs. Looking at puppies as young as seven to eight weeks it is possible to see the angulation of the fore and hindquarters. The shoulders should be well laid back and placed well under the body,

Expression is an important feature and this Rottweiler typifies the noble look of the breed.

The black outer coat should look glossy, and the tan markings should be a rich rust or mahogany.

with elbows close-fitting and not loose. The line of the back from withers to croup should be level, with no dip or slope, and the croup is very slightly sloping, with the (docked) tail carried horizontally or slightly above the horizontal when the dog is alert. In some countries docking is forbidden by law and it has been found that the tail carriage varies.

When viewed from the front the forelegs should be straight – they should turn neither in nor out. Viewed from the side the pasterns should slope slightly forward in order to allow then to act as 'shock absorbers' during movement.

The hindquarters should be powerful and well-muscled. The stifle joint should not be over-angulated – dogs with this fault often stand (or are placed by their handlers in the show ring) with the hind legs stretched out behind, nor should the stifle be too straight, which results in a short stride.

Dewclaws should always be removed from the hindlegs by the veterinarian when the puppies are around two days old, but dewclaws on the front legs may be left on if desired. (I prefer all dewclaws to be removed so there is no danger of injury through being caught in any obstacle.)

CHOOSING A PUPPY

Choosing a puppy from a litter all of which are the same colour is far from easy, and apart from appearance, it is vital that attention is paid to character. The dominant dog in a litter is not suited to a sedentary life, but needs an active owner who will give plenty of companionship and stimulation. The quieter puppy is better to a first-time Rottweiler owner or someone who prefers a more sedate youngster to occupy the family's days, while the shy, nervous puppy should not be chosen.

Explain carefully what you want and put your trust in the breeder, for it takes years to be able to evaluate dogs against the breed standard, and predicting which puppies in a litter will be 'fliers', those likely to develop into potential show winners, is extremely difficult even for an expert.

From time to time, new owners decide after they have purchased a pet puppy that they would like to show him, and then they are disappointed when the dog is not placed in competition. Of course, puppies sold as pets have become Champions, but it happens only rarely. In general, you get what you pay for, so do not be disappointed if your pet is exactly that – a delightful family dog, not quite up to show standard. Enjoy him, and next time around, order a show prospect from your chosen breeder.

Chapter Eight

HEALTH CARE

Rottweilers have a life span of around ten years; large breeds do not live as long as small breeds, alas. However, good food, regular exercise and clean, comfortable living conditions contribute to keeping your dog healthy. Viewed from an entirely financial perspective, it makes sense to have a healthy dog; an unhealthy one can prove to be expensive in veterinarian's fees.

GENERAL CARE

GROOMING
Rottweilers have 'easicare' coats and although they shed their coats, this process is quickly over. The ideal grooming schedule is a quick daily comb and brush. If this is not possible, aim for two or three times a week, but daily when your dog is shedding his coat.
My preference is to use a horse's dandy brush of natural bristle, and a small rake comb, which removes any dead hair. Start to brush (and only brush) your Rottweiler puppy from day one. The puppy will probably not like it at first, but persevere, as he must become accustomed to being groomed from a young age.

NAILS
These should be kept short; if they are allowed to become too long they can cause the feet to splay, predisposing them to injury. Clip the nail with guiltotine style clippers, but make sure you only remove the tip of the nail, otherwise bleeding and pain will result. Alternatively, file the nails with a carpenter's file until a small area of grey/white is visible in the centre of the nail – then stop!

TEETH
Tartar must not be allowed to accumulate on the teeth, not only does it smell offensive, but it can cause gum disease. If you give your Rottweiler the occcasional marrow bone or hard biscuits to chew, it will prevent tartar forming. There are also special toothpaste and toothbrushes available for dogs.

BATHING
Bathing a dog should not be done more than is absolutely necessary, as too much immersion can cause the coat to become dry. See that the bath water is only tepid (test it by immersing your elbow), dry the dog off thoroughly, and if a bath has to be given in cold weather, keep him indoors for a couple of hours to dry off thoroughly.

Good food, regular exercise, and clean, comfortable living conditions will help to keep your dog healthy.

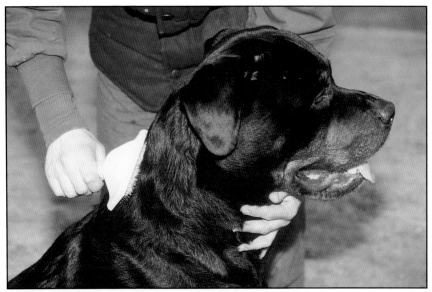

The Rottweiler's coat is easy to care for.

A quick daily comb and brush is the ideal grooming schedule, and this becomes essential when your dog is shedding his coat. Regular grooming will ensure that the coat is kept clean.

CHOOSING A VET

Great care should be taken in your choice of veterinarian. Visit several practices to enquire about the services offered: are there any partners who specialise in small animals? Are home visits made? Are referrals to clinicians willingly given, if this proves necessary? *Most important of all:* is there any prejudice against Rottweilers in the practice? (It does happen!)

WHEN TO CONSULT YOUR VET

1. If there is any rapid loss of weight.
2. If your Rottweiler starts to drink excessively, except, of course, in very hot weather.
3. If your dog's breath begins to smell strongly.
4. If there is sickness and diarrhoea lasting more than twenty-four hours.
5. If there is bleeding from the penis or discharge from the vulva between seasons.
6. If your Rottweiler is lame and the condition persists beyond a few days.
7. If there is any marked change in behaviour.

CONTAGIOUS DISEASES

Apart from the owner's contribution mentioned above, there are other factors which must be taken into account. First and foremost, every Rottweiler puppy *must* have a course of injections to protect him against the potentially lethal contagious diseases: distemper, leptospirosis, hepatitis and parvovirus, followed by an annual booster injection. It is emphasised that it is essential to give these injections throughout the life of the dog as a preventive measure. In some countries, such as the USA, rabies inoculations are required by law.

INHERITED DISEASES

HIP DYSPLASIA

Orthopaedic problems are high on the list of conditions which affect the larger breeds. The most common of these is hip dysplasia, an inherited condition in which the hip joint, a ball-and-socket joint, is malformed. The degree of unsoundness and discomfort depends on the extent of the malformation. In severe cases, surgical intervention may be needed in order to alleviate the pain.

It is impossible for any breeder to be certain that a puppy will not develop hip dysplasia, but the chances are considerably reduced if the parents are X-rayed through an official Kennel Club scheme or some other reliable agency, and have a low score. Not so many dogs (or humans!) have perfectly formed hips, and very minor deviations have little or no effect on soundness. While hip dysplasia is an inherited disease, the environment also plays a part, and no Rottweiler puppy should be allowed to become overweight, play on slippery surfaces like tiles or polished floors, or run up and downstairs while he is growing.

OSTEOCHONDROSIS

Osteochondrosis is considered by some clinicians to be the most common cause of lameness in the young dog of the larger breeds. It is a disease of growing cartilage which fails to turn into bone. Cracks appear, and sometimes pieces of the joint flake off. There are varying degrees of pain and unsoundness, and the condition is found in the shoulder, elbow, hock and stifle. Rottweilers are most frequently affected in the elbow.

If a puppy becomes lame, he should be rested (not always so easy!), and if he is still lame after a week, he should be checked by a veterinarian, who may refer you to a clinician for further investigation. Surgery may be advised, depending on the severity of the condition. While there is not yet general agreement, osteochondrosis is thought to be an inherited problem.

RUPTURE OF CRUCIATE LIGAMENTS
The bones of the knee (stifle joint) are held together by several cruciate ligaments, and rupture of the anterior ligament is a common problem in the heavier breeds, occurring very often in dogs under the age of three years. At first the ligament stretches, causing the knee joint to become unstable, and eventually it ruptures. The dog may not show any initial lameness, but as the ligament stretches, then ruptures, the dog will become unsound.

From the time the joint becomes unstable, osteoarthritis starts to develop. If the ligament is not repaired, the arthritis worsens, so the earlier surgery is carried out, the better for the dog. After the operation, which is usually extremely successful, a most carefully controlled regime of exercise is necessary.

For approximately one month, the dog must go into the garden *on lead* for toileting only, then on lead for a distance of 100-300 yards for a further month, and after that *gradually* increasing the distance, carefully monitoring progress. Make haste slowly is the golden rule. If the owner does not, the best of surgeon's work will have been in vain. Certain bloodlines seem to be affected more than others, and dogs which have been operated on should not be bred from.

EYE PROBLEMS
The most common eye disease is entropion, where the eyelid(s) turn inwards. This causes 'runny' eyes, sets up inflammation, and may cause ulceration of the cornea, which is extremely painful. While it usually occurs in dogs with a lot of loose skin on the head, this is not always so. Although entropion sometimes occurs as a secondary condition, it is usually considered to be an inherited problem, which must be referred to a veterinarian quickly. It is cruel not to have the condition corrected surgically, and this is quite a simple operation. Dogs with this problem should not be used for breeding.

Should your Rottweiler develop 'runny' eyes, consult a veterinarian, as often all that is needed is ointment to be applied two or three times a day for a week to ten days.

SKIN PROBLEMS
Dogs which scratch continually should be checked for the presence of fleas, which are all too easy to pick up, or other parasites, and a suitable spray or shampoo should be obtained from the veterinarian. You should also use a powder on all surfaces with which the dog is in contact, and wash bedding. Treating the dog without dealing with the contact surfaces is a waste of time. There will only be reinfestation. Scratching erodes the outer layer of the skin which means infection can gain entry. There is inflammation, and pustules form (oedema), and, therefore, persistent scratching needs to be investigated.

It is important to choose a vet that you can talk to – and one that gets on with Rottweilers!

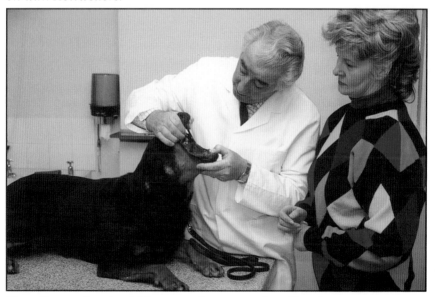

Your Rottweiler should be trained to accept handling by strangers.

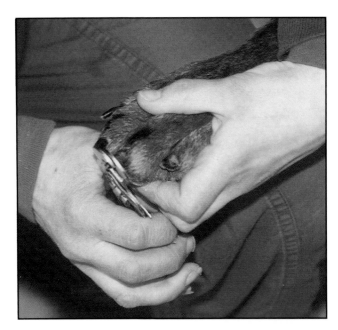

Nails should be kept short: they can be clipped using guillotine style clippers.

Teeth should be kept clean by giving your Rottweiler a marrow bone or hard biscuits to chew, or you can clean them with a toothbrush, using specially manufactured dog toothpaste.

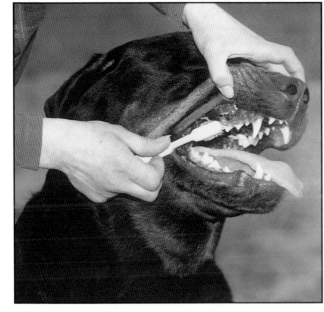

Rottweilers sometimes suffer from 'hot spots' which appear overnight as large wet patches, often on the head or neck, which are extremely painful and itchy. An injection and tablets from the veterinarian effect a cure, but it is essential to stop the dog scratching the affected area, so it may be necessary to use a preventative measure, such as a 'bucket' (with the base removed, and fastened with a collar round the neck).

Skin irritation may also be caused by a food allergy, and to be certain which food is causing the problem requires careful investigation by a veterinarian, utilising an eliminative diet.

Little is currently known about the cause of dermatitis. If the dog is kept in a kennel, the type of disinfectant used to clean kennel and run may be implicated. Inside the home, the possibilities include: dyes or stains used on flooring, floor cleaners, carpet shampoos, plastic bowls and rubber mats, to name but a few. Outside the home it could be attributed to: herbicides, pine needles, wood chips, wet cement, and plants of all kinds. If the problem does not clear up quickly after consultation with your veterinarian, ask for a referral to a veterinary dermatologist.

BLOAT AND GASTRIC TORSION
Bloat is a condition most often found in medium-sized and large deep-bodied dogs, that usually occurs shortly after feeding when the stomach rapidly fills with gas, swelling up and sometimes also twisting (gastric torsion). The dog is in great pain, has difficulty in breathing, retches but cannot vomit, and is greatly distressed. This is a Grade One emergency and if your dog 'blows', telephone your veterinarian to say you are bringing the dog over immediately. Even seconds may mean the difference between life and death. This condition is a 'killer'. Various causes are thought to contribute to this condition, such as consuming dry food followed by copious drinking, vigorous exercise too soon after a meal, food fermenting in the stomach, overloading the stomach, and swallowing an abnormal amount of air, which can be the case with greedy, rapid eaters.

Some breeds are especially susceptible e.g. Bloodhounds and Irish Wolfhounds, but it does occur in Rottweilers sometimes. It is better to check a false alarm than have the dog suffer an agonising death.

CANCER
Unfortunately, cancer is far from uncommon in Rottweilers, and bone cancer (osteosarcoma) is probably the most prevalent. With the increasing sophistication of veterinary medicine, treatments such as chemotherapy and radiotherapy are available at some veterinary colleges, and techniques are improving all the time. However, some types of cancer are not amenable to treatment and there is no alternative but euthanasia.

INTERNAL PARASITES (WORMS)
Throughout their lives, dogs should be wormed at regular intervals of three to six months, for the sake of the animal's health, and that of its human family. There are three main types of worms, round (the most common), hook and tape, and there are preparations, obtainable from a veterinarian – not 'over the counter' – which will deal with all three parasites at once. Worms are easily picked up through sniffing faeces of other dogs, eating affected meat, and through flea infestation.

While there is a risk of children being infected by roundworm larvae, this is a remote possibility if regular wormings are carried out. Of course, no dog should be allowed to lick a child's face or hands, and children should be supervised so that they always wash their hands after touching dogs or being licked by them.

In certain countries, e.g. USA and Australia, another type of parasite, heartworm, is found. Treatment for this is slightly different, for the dog must be given a tablet daily or monthly, at the direction of the veterinarian, as a preventative.

EUTHANASIA
When a Rottweiler has given pleasure to his owner and family, and the sad time comes when his quality of life is no longer good, the dog should be put to sleep, preferably in his own home, in the owner's arms, while the owner is talking to him to reassure. However painful this may be to the owner, it is the last kindness you can do for a loyal companion, and it is one you should never 'duck'.

Chapter Nine

BREEDING

When pet owners say they would like to breed from a bitch, I usually say "Don't"! There are so many aspects, not normally appreciated, which should be considered carefully, and I want to write a little about them.

COUNTING THE COST
First of all, forget the notion that there is money to be made out of breeding Rottweilers. There is not. Obvious expenses include: extra food for the bitch during pregnancy, feeding the puppies once they are weaned, and advertising the litter, as well as the cost of the stud fee.

So called 'hidden costs' include veterinary charges if there are complications during pregnancy or whelping; the cost of keeping puppies beyond the age of seven to eight weeks, for not all go to their new homes then, and this is the cost not only in money, because their appetites are increasing as they grow but also in time, for the puppies *must* start to be socialised; and finally, the possible refund or part-refund of the purchase price if the puppy develops a condition which makes it unfit for the purpose for which it was purchased.

RESPONSIBILITIES OF THE BREEDER
It must be stressed that a breeder's responsibility for the puppies he has bred continues throughout their lives. All potential owners must be checked out to ensure they want a Rottweiler for the right reasons (not as a guard in a yard, or to enhance a would-be macho image) and are sensible people who will ensure the puppy is socialised and trained.

A breeder should be prepared to take back any stock which, for one reason or another, the original purchaser is unable to keep. A breeder should be knowledgeable about canine matters generally, and the Rottweiler breed in particular, so he can advise purchasers on rearing, training, socialisation and any problems that may arise during the early days when a puppy goes to its new owner, who may never have had a Rottweiler before.

ASSESSING THE BITCH
If, despite all these factors, an owner decides he still wants to have a litter, and he has the time and space to keep the puppies, there remains the vital consideration: is the bitch a good example of the breed, both in appearance in temperament, as well as being free from inherited problems such as hip dysplasia, osteochondrosis, or entropion? No bitch with these conditions should be used for breeding, however

The stud dog must complement your bitch; he should be free from hereditary disorders and have a sound temperament.

beautiful she is, or how good her temperament. These conditions will only be perpetuated, and they can cause much suffering not only to the dog, but also worry and upset to the owners.

So far, so good? Next think about the accommodation for the bitch and puppies. If she lives indoors as a house pet, she will not take kindly to being shut in a kennel or shed with the puppies. Many a bitch has had her whelping box in the kitchen or another room which has been cleared for the event. However, if she is a kennel dog, ensure the kennel is warm and insulated with an infra red lamp hung over the whelping box. The puppies must be kept in a temperature of 75 degrees Fahrenheit for at least the first week of life, whether they are in a kennel, or in a house.

CHOOSING A STUD DOG

Choice of stud dog is crucially important, and it should be made on the basis of what is suited to the bitch, being totally realistic about her shortcomings as well as her virtues, not on the proximity of the dog to your home, or solely on a dog's show record. Look around at dog shows, visit kennels, check pedigrees, and ensure that the temperament of the proposed mate is excellent, in other words he is outgoing, friendly and intelligent. He should have good hips, and not have been operated on or suffer from osteochondrosis or entropion.

MATING

A Rottweiler bitch should not be mated until she is two years of age by which time she is physically and mentally mature. If the owner of the stud dog is not experienced (they usually are), arrange to take an experienced person with you to help. Note that the bitch always travels to the dog. Insist on staying with your bitch while she is mated, and remember that if a dog is proved, that is he has sired puppies already, the stud fee is paid at the time of mating. If he is unproven, the fee is paid when the litter is born. Clarify with the dog's owner that if the bitch misses, a repeat mating will be given.

PREGNANCY

It is sometimes difficult to tell whether a bitch is in whelp or not, until quite late on, especially if she is a large bitch, but some veterinarians have equipment to give a 'scan' in order to reveal if a bitch is in whelp, and how many puppies she is carrying. A pregnant bitch will require more food and vitamins/mineral supplements if she and the puppies are to be fit and healthy, but she must not be allowed to become fat. Assuming she is normally fed twice a day, morning and evening, give an extra meal at midday from the sixth week after mating. Exercise is important to keep her fit, but she must not be allowed to rush about or play games with other dogs. Bitches carry their pups for sixty-three days, but a bitch can whelp a few days early or late. Never allow a bitch to be more than three days overdue without having her checked by your veterinarian. Accustom the bitch to her whelping box and quarters a week or so before the expected birth.

In the later stages of pregnancy some bitches can become very 'clingy', perhaps needing reassurance. A bitch may also be very restless, wandering about digging holes outside, or even in the house. Such behaviour is perfectly natural. The day before whelping the bitch will be extremely restless, often refusing food, and her temperature will drop from 101 degrees Fahrenheit to between 98 and 99 degrees.

PREPARING FOR THE WHELPING

ITEMS REQUIRED
1. A whelping box, long enough for the bitch to lie full length, and wide enough for the bitch and puppies to 'spread out', with guard rails all round, so puppies can crawl out of her way and not get crushed.
2. Three pieces of washable bedding (one in use, two spare) to fit exactly the whelping box.
3. Clean, *old* towels for drying off puppies (new towels are unsuitable as lint comes off).
4. Cotton wool (cotton). You will need little blobs to wipe pups' eyes and noses, and some squares taken off a big roll, in case it is necessary to help with a breech birth.
5. A pair of blunt-nosed scissors.
6. Disinfectant.
7. A mug in which to place scissors and diluted disinfectant.
8. Glucose.
9. Coagulant to control bleeding.
10. A cardboard box with blanket or towel, and a covered hot-water bottle, or a heated pad for earliest born pups, if necessary, otherwise they may run the risk of being crushed as later ones are born.
11. Pencil and paper to 'log' births i.e. time and whether placenta delivered or not.

WHELPING
After the first stage of restlessness and panting, the actual whelping may start very suddenly. Contractions begin, the muscular tension of the bitch's body from shoulders to tail is exerted, and any time after this a puppy should arrive. A maiden bitch may be bewildered by the arrival of puppies, not knowing what to do, so the owner should tear open the membranous sac containing puppy and fluid, and wipe the puppy's mouth and nostrils dry. This must be done quickly, otherwise the puppy can drown.

If the bitch does not bite through the umbilical cord, the owner should deal with this too. Pinch the cord between the fingers about 1 1/2 inches from the puppy's abdomen, and then cut it with the scissors which have been soaking in disinfectant. Apply a spot of coagulant on cotton wool to the end of the cord if it is very bloody.

Puppies are born at varying intervals. Veterinary assistance *must* be sought immediately if the bitch strains for two hours without producing a puppy, as one may be wedged across the birth canal and help is required urgently to save it, and any other puppies waiting to be born. If the whelping is lengthy, offer the bitch some milk with a little added glucose.

Most Rottweiler whelpings are trouble free, although this must never be taken for granted. A bitch should *never* be left alone to 'get on with it' as there is always the risk of losing the bitch and her pups.

WHEN TO CALL THE VET
1. If the bitch shows a dark-green discharge before or during whelping.
2. If the bedding is very wet and the bitch just sits looking listless and bewildered (uterine inertia).
3. If no puppies are produced after two hours of contractions.

Do not breed with your bitch unless she is a good example of the breed, both in appearance and temperament, and she must be free from inherited problems.

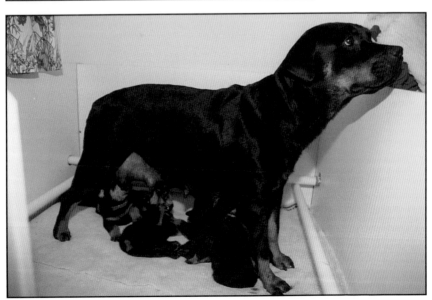

Resist the temptation of inviting visitors to inspect the new litter, as this could be unsettling for the bitch.

For the first few days, the bitch will cater for all the puppies' needs, cleaning them and feeding them.

Weaning starts from two-and-a-half to three weeks, depending on the size of the litter.

4. If a puppy is too large to be expelled – just part of it protruding.

5. If there is no sign of pups by the sixty-sixth day, veterinary intervention is essential to preserve the lives of the bitch and her pups.

6. Check before and after whelping that the bitch's milk glands have not become inflamed and hardened.

7. Eclampsia: this condition does not happen very often, but it is important that the breeder is aware of it. Eclampsia is due to excessive depletion of the calcium store in lactating bitches. Symptoms are hysterical excitement and continuous panting. All puppies should be taken away from the bitch, and the veterinarian must be called immediately. *This is an emergency.*

POST-WHELPING
After the litter has arrived, encourage your bitch to go outside and relieve herself (she may take a bit of persuading!) Your veterinarian must check her the day after whelping, regardless of whether the whelping was trouble free or not.

For two to three days after whelping, the bitch should be fed a light diet of milk and glucose, scrambled eggs, some rice pudding, or a little cereal and milk. She will need lots of fluids while feeding the litter – not just water, which should always be available. The total food intake must be increased as the puppies grow, being divided into three to four meals daily.

A litter of newborn puppies is very appealing, and owners understandably want to show them off to friends and neighbours. Resist the temptation for the first three weeks as it is most unfair on the bitch to subject her and the puppies to visits, however well intentioned, not to mention the risk of infection.

WEANING
Start to wean at about two-and-a-half weeks if the litter is large, otherwise three weeks, giving milky feeds, then a baby food, and then finely-scraped, good quality meat. Check the puppies' claws at two weeks and, if necessary, trim them, because it is excruciatingly painful for a bitch's underside to be scratched by 'needle points'.

Puppies should be wormed with a preparation from the veterinarian at four weeks, and the dose should be repeated in ten to fourteen days, or as advised. After the bitch has finished with the litter, she should also be wormed, as she was before mating.

Bitches enjoy playing with their puppies, and for the pups this is an essential part of the growing-up process of 'learning to be dogs'. However, by the time the puppies are four to six weeks old, a bitch needs to get away from the demands of her brood for some peace and quiet. Ensure that she can do this. This is only a brief outline of what is involved in breeding a litter, and owners should read one of the many good books devoted to the subject for a fuller understanding.

SELLING THE PUPPIES
When the time comes for the puppies to go to their new homes at seven to eight weeks, check out every prospective owner as, hopefully, you were checked, for suitability to own a Rottweiler. A potential owner must have a securely fenced garden; someone must be home for most or all of the day, and the owner must have a firm, sensible character, so necessary when owning a Rottweiler.

Discuss fully the needs of a Rottweiler – exercise, socialisation, and problems that may arise through incorrect understanding and handling. When the puppy is collected, you should give the new owner: a pedigree, a Kennel Club registration (if ready), a diet sheet, information about wormings and inoculations, and emphasise that you want to be kept informed of the puppy's progress. If no contact is made after the puppy has been in the new home for a week, telephone yourself and find out how the puppy is settling.

Rottweilers enjoy the mental stimulation of competing in Agility contests.

Chapter Ten

FUN WITH YOUR ROTTWEILER

Research has shown that owning a dog is good for us. We take exercise which we might otherwise not do; stroking pets helps us to relax, lowering stress levels; and we gain pleasure from looking after another living creature.('nurturing effect'). These considerations apart, there are other ways in which we may enjoy our pets if we wish.

DOG SHOWS
Shows are held under the auspices of the Kennel Clubs of various countries; dogs compete against each other, the winners being those who, in the opinion of the judge, most closely fit the Breed Standard, the 'blueprint' for the breed.

Being a popular breed, entries in Rottweiler classes are high, and an owner should seek advice from the breeder concerning the dog's chances, as there is no point in wasting time and money entering shows if the dog is not of show quality. Indeed, the prospective owner should try to decide whether he wants to show his Rottweiler before he buys a puppy, and then go to a reputable breeder with a proven record of success in the show ring and whose stock he likes.

Your Rottweiler must be in show condition – fit, well-muscled and well-groomed – in order to compete with the best.

There is a difference in price between those puppies the breeder considers to be potential show specimens, and those of pet quality. It is impossible to decide with certainty at seven to eight weeks of age whether a puppy will be a show winner, and anyone who says they are able to do so is either an incurable optimist or an inveterate liar!

Dog showing can be expensive in money (entry fees and travel costs), and time. It also demands a certain hardiness of spirit in order to be able to accept disappointments gracefully (when you think your dog should have been placed and it is not), and not to indulge in petty criticism and back biting, unfortunately all too often found.

But if you want 'to have a go', start off at a small informal show, advertised in the dog and local press, which is an invaluable introduction to the sport, then graduate to the 'serious' world of Championship shows. It goes without saying that before entering a show the owner should ensure that his dog is in show condition. Your Rottweiler should be carrying just the right amount of weight (neither too fat or too thin), the nails should be trimmed if necessary, and the coat should be well groomed, glossy and clean. The eyes should be clear and not 'runny', and the teeth should also be clean, with no deposits of tartar visible. Finally, the dog should be what we term 'fit', having been exercised daily to ensure he has well-developed muscles. To be a successful exhibitor demands not only a good dog, but also a competent handler. Most towns have dog training clubs with special classes for ring training, and both you and your dog will learn a lot from attending these before you attempt to compete in the show ring.

TYPES OF SHOWS
BRITAIN
In the UK, there is a variety of different shows: Exemption (usually fund-raising events; dogs do not have to be registered with the Kennel Club), Limited/Sanction and Primary (excluding dogs which have won higher awards, thus giving puppies and young stock a chance to be placed), but the two most frequently held are Open and Championship shows.

OPEN SHOWS: Any dog may enter, including Champions. These shows may be quite small or approach the size of a Championship show, but classes are restricted according to the age and amount of winning a dog has done, so the beginner has a chance to win a placing with his dog.

CHAMPIONSHIP SHOWS: A general Championship show has a large classification for breeds, most of which are allocated one set of Kennel Club Challenge Certificates – this is the only type of show where these are on offer. When a dog or a bitch has won three Challenge Certificates under three different judges, then the dog will become a Champion. As a Champion, a dog may still compete at shows, and some go on to win a large number of CCs before they are retired from the ring.

AMERICA
MATCHES: The local All Breed and Specialty Clubs will probably hold one or two matches a year. These are advertised in the 'dog Press', giving details of breeds, classes and judges. Entries are made on the morning of the show. Judges are often

aspiring to become Championship show judges of the breed. Classes usually range from Puppy through Novice on to Open. Sometimes the classes are for mixed sexes, or in the case of Specialty matches, most classes will be divided by sex. Champions are not eligible for matches.

CHAMPIONSHIP SHOWS: These can be for all breeds, selected breeds, or one breed. They are advertised in the 'dog Press'. Premiums are sent to all intending exhibitors. After the closing date for entries, passes, catalog numbers and schedules are sent to exhibitors. Points are awarded towards the Championship title by a judge who is approved by the Kennel Club. A total of fifteen points under three separate judges must be gained for a dog to become a Champion, including two 'majors' under separate judges (3, 4 or 5 point wins).

SPECIALTIES: These are held annually or bi-annually by the club concerned, usually attracting large entries. Again, Championship points are awarded. The judge is normally someone held in high esteem by breeders and exhibitors, and sometimes an overseas judge recieves an invitation to judge.

WORKING EVENTS

Rottweilers are a working breed, and there are several activities for which they can be trained, where they perform with credit. These events are Working Trials, Obedience, and Agility. The first of these is the one where the Rottweiler really excels. Dogs have to negotiate jumps (scale, long jump, hurdle), track (follow the scent of the tracklayer who has left articles for the dog to find), search (for articles left in a square), and do control exercises such as heeling, sit/down, stay, retrieving a dumb-bell etc. Training your Rottweiler to carry out these exercises is hard work, but it is very rewarding, deepening the bond between owner and dog.

In Obedience competitions the dog is not required to jump, track or search, performing instead control and scent discrimination exercises in a very precise and accurate manner. While Rottweilers have done quite well in this type of event, they can become bored with the precision which is needed to achieve top placings, being more suited to the wider scope offered by Working Trials.

Agility is the latest of the working events to be organised and a few Rottweilers have achieved good results, but it must be said that it is far from easy for the heavier breeds to wrest placings from the lighter and faster breeds like Border Collies. Dogs have to negotiate a series of obstacles, jumps of different types, a 'tunnel', raised platform and weaving poles, and the winner is the dog incurring the fewest penalties and completing the course in the fastest time. It is very much a spectator sport, most exciting to watch, and the dogs really enjoy it, setting a cracking pace. To participate, both dogs *and* handlers have to be fit, although the latter do not have to negotiate the obstacles!

Anyone interested in learning more about Trials, Obedience or Agility and where training classes are held may obtain details from the national Kennel Clubs in the countries where these competitions are available. Regular training for all three types of event is essential.

THERAPY DOGS

It is only within the last few years that the benefits which pets of all kinds confer on

Rottweiler have achieved good results in Agility competitions, although they are not as quick as the smaller, lighter breeds.

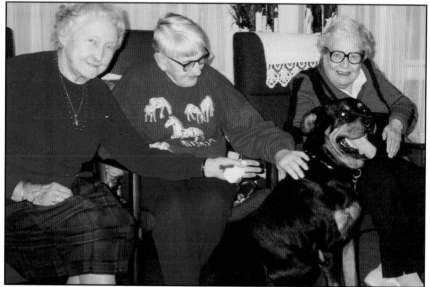

'Lottie', a former 'rescue' dog, is now a much-loved Therapy dog, giving pleasure to all those she visits.

Back-packing with your dog is a popular pastime in countries such as Norway. Here, tail-docking is banned.

Carting is a popular hobby with Rottweiler enthusuasts, and has proved a very successful way of collecting money for charity.

their owners have been officially recognised. Hospitals, nursing homes, and schools for handicapped children receive visits from owners and their dogs. Many elderly, long-stay patients have had to part with much-loved pets when they entered hospital and miss them badly, so the canine visitors bring back happy memories. Therapy Dogs are officially assessed for suitability, as a dog which is excitable, nervous or disobedient would not fit in.

Those Rottweilers which make visits have been extremely successful: gentle with the elderly and patient with children, enjoying all the attention they receive.

CARTING
Carting events are organised in the USA and South Africa, and in South Africa a dog can become a Carting Champion if he wins three Carting Certificates under three different judges.

Before the dog is hitched to the cart, some basic control exercises (heel, recall and stay) must be carried out with the dog on lead in the Novice class, and off lead in the Senior class. Once hitched to the cart, the dog has to haul forward at normal, fast and slow paces, and stop, back up, and stay. In the Senior class the cart carries a load and more complicated manoeuvres are performed.

In the UK it is forbidden by law to permit a dog to pull a cart on a public highway, but there is nothing to prevent carting competitions taking place on private ground. Events are often scheduled with prizes for the best decorated carts, and dogs pulling carts are used to collect for charity at fetes and agricultural shows. In the US dogs pull carts (sometimes with a passenger on board) at parades and processions, and they always attract a lot of attention.

HERDING
In the US herding competitions are held for several different breeds including the Rottweiler, but in the UK sheepdog trials are confined to sheepdogs. However, with the increases in leisure time available, it is to be hoped that these events may be staged at some time in the future.

RESCUE WORK
In mountainous or heavily forested areas dogs are often called upon to find missing people, and my experience of Rottweilers in Norway showed that they are competent in this work and enjoy it. Doubtless Rottweilers would make good rescue dogs almost anywhere.

COMPANION DOGS
Of course, many owners have no desire to do anything other than enjoy the rewarding companionship of their Rottweiler. In order to get the best out of his dog, the owner must ensure that he is well-socialised as a puppy, trained to be well-mannered and obedient and, last but by no means least, the dog must be a good car traveller, since car ownership amongst Rottweiler owners is high!

While not all dogs are car sick, a distressing problem, taking trouble over car acclimatisation is well worthwhile. Take the puppy out in the car (not on a full stomach) for very short distances, as often as possible. The car should be associated with pleasant happenings, so feed your puppy in a stationary car, or finish a car trip with a walk or a game. Some puppies need to be given a travel sickness remedy to help overcome sickness or drooling. Do not hesitate to seek advice because once a puppy or adult associates a car with being sick, it will drool or be sick in it even when the car is stationary. Every effort should be made to prevent such an association from forming.

Going out in a car without a Rottweiler – without any dog for that matter – always seems to make the journey a lonely affair. Only very hot weather makes me leave my dogs behind, even if the journey is just to the shops a couple of miles away!

Opinions are divided on the advisability of having a dog guard in the car. There is a dog harness now available, and also fitted cages, which are useful for restless dogs, who could create potentially dangerous situations by disturbing the driver.

A final word about car travel. In hot, even warm weather, the interior of a car, even with windows down, can quickly become like a furnace, causing suffering and an agonising death for any dog left in such conditions. The dog literally cooks. Do not just take my word for it; put a thermometer in the car on a hot day and see for yourself. Leaving the vehicle in the shade on a hot day is no guarantee of a dog's comfort or safety, so please be warned.

DOGS AND CHILDREN

It is important that your Rottweiler gets on with children, even if they are not part of his human family. However, a happy relationship does not just happen, and certain house rules are necessary. In the case of a baby, remember that the strange cries may alarm the dog, and so the dog should be introduced to the new arrival when the baby is not crying or screaming. Disrupt the dog's normal routine as little as possible; allow the dog to be around when the baby is fed, changed, or bathed, and try to take your dog out with the baby for a stroll, once he is accustomed to the new arrival.

Once the baby starts to crawl and investigate, care must be taken to ensure that the dog is not poked, pulled about or otherwise pestered. Toddlers, of course, have no conception of right or wrong and must be taught to respect the dog – an on-going process which is not accomplished overnight. Have a playpen for the toddler and an outside run for the dog, where it is is on its own and secure when an adult is not present to supervise. A rule to follow without fail is: *Never leave a young child (or children) alone with a dog of any breed.* To do so is unfair on both child and dog. An adult must always be present, for you can never be sure what children will do: they can be too rough with young puppies and thoughtless and provoking with older dogs.

On occasion, even the best behaved of children can try to show off with a Rottweiler, getting him to bark or jump up on friends. This must never be allowed to happen. When children are playing rough, noisy games with their friends, keep the dog out of the way for it may well misinterpret what is going on.No dog of a large, strong breed should be taken out by a child under the age of sixteen. This is to protect both dog and child because it is impossible to predict what kind of situation is likely to arise – loose, aggressive dogs, with or without an accompanying owner, other children attempting to tease the dog, and situations the dog has not encountered before. A child does not have the physical strength to hold a Rottweiler or any other large dog if it becomes excited, or if it is attacked by another dog.

Rottweilers are very fun-loving and playful dogs. Care and commonsense from the outset will make sure your dog and your child have an enjoyable relationship.

As children get older they can help to care for the dog, but they should never be allowed to take the dog outside unsupervised.

CONCLUSION

Much has already been written about the Rottweiler, and in this short book I have tried to do justice to a great breed whose qualities make him outstanding as a companion and protector of home and family, as well as a working dog.

Nothing is accomplished without effort, and I should like to end with the words of an American friend who said so rightly: "A dog is not good at knowing what to do, only what he is taught to do." Give your Rottweiler affection and kindness. Take the trouble to train and guide him. Your reward will be loyalty and companionship all the days of his life.